Highland Chronicle

Ardkinglass Campbells, Livingstons, Erskines and Callanders

Robert Lindsay

ISBN: Softcover   978-1-9845-0207-0
         Hardcover   978-1-9845-0208-7
         EBook   978-1-9845-0209-4

Print information available on the last page

Rev. date: 09/19/2018

To order additional copies of this book, contact:
Xlibris
1-800-455-039
www.xlibris.com.au
Orders@Xlibris.com.au

Highland Chronicle

To the inhabitants on the shores of Loch Fyne and Loch Goil

FOREWORD

Why does anyone write about the Highland past? I think the great writers can explain it.

Neil Munro said: "The things we love intensely are the things worth writing about. I could never keep Inveraray out of any story of mine, and I never will… a small field to till it may be said, but I know better. This parish, though you may not think it, is a miniature of the world".

I was brought up on the shores of Loch Fyne; staring across the loch to the beautiful town of Inveraray. When I return from foreign places to Loch Fyne, I am reminded of Neil Munro's description in "John Splendid" when he and his friend, Elrigmore returned from battle to Loch Fyne. To savour the moment they wait until a cloud has passed over the sun and then they caste their eyes upon

"Loch Fyne stretching out before us, a spread of twinkling silver waves…. and the yellow light of the early year gilded the remotest hills of Ardno and Ben Ime….the town revealed but its higher chimneys and the gable of the kirk still its smoke told of occupation; the castle frowned as of old, and overall Dunchuach".

I write this book to recall the fond memories of childhood.

This is the story of a notable family whose clan members had a large influence on Scottish political and social affairs being advisers to monarchs, and as soldiers and legal advocates on the national stage. It is, a pastiche of highland characters: James Callendar, the Erskine brothers, Elspeth and Niall Campbell and Hopie MacArthur.

Plutarch said: "By the study of their biographies, we receive each more as a guest into our minds, and we seem to understand their character as a result of a personal acquaintance, because we have obtained from their acts, the best and most important means of forming an opinion about them. What greater pleasure could'st thou gain than this? What more valuable for the elevation of our own character?"

This is also a personal history because, through the accident of birth and circumstance, I have gained a personal acquaintance with their actions and hope in this way to bring for a brief moment their ghosts back to life.

— Robert Erskine Lindsay

CONTENTS

CHAPTER 1
THE CAMPBELL WARRIORS
OF ARDKINGLASS

As one drives westwards from Glasgow—passing through Arrochar, climbing Glen Croe, and going over the Rest and Be Thankful—the past comes to mind; the same Campbell family owned this vast highland tract for more than 640 years. From at least 1396 until the estate was sold in 1905, the Campbells of Ardkinglass owned the area reaching from Arrochar to Glen Croe, Glen Kinglass, Loch Goil, and the land— including the fishing—around Loch Fyne. This included the castle of Dunderave on the west side of Loch Fyne and up to Strachur on the east side.[1]

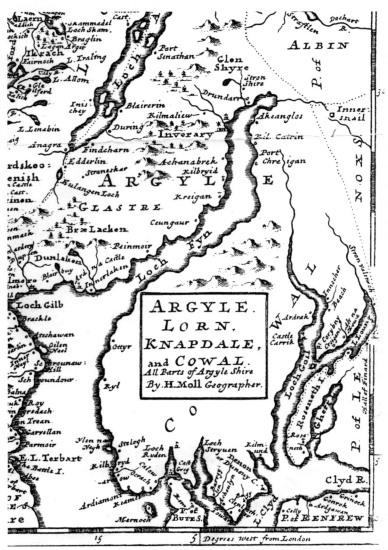

Map of Loch Goil and Loch Fyne (Fin) 1725,
showing Ardkinglass (Akeagles), St Catherine's (Kil Catrine).

The Three Holy Brethren

Originally the Campbell lairds were buried at the Lochgoilhead church, known as the Church of the Three Holy Brethren, who were thought to be three Irish saints. At the east end is a heraldically decorated Campbell of Ardkinglass tomb. It is is mentioned in papal letters in 1379. In the adjoining house is a fine ten-foot tall obelisk sundial, dated 1626, with the initials of the tenth laird and his wife, Helen Maxwell, who had a manor house there.[2]

Church of the Three Holy Brethren (Loch Goil) being original burial place of Ardkinglass Campbells.

A heraldic emblem in the Interior of the Three Holy Brethren church (Loch Goil) Crest of 4th Laird and Buchanan being his wife's family in 1512. Died at Flodden.

Another heraldic emblem in the Interior of the Three Holy Brethren church (Loch Goil) Here lies James Campbell (6th laird). DGMM is Deo Gratas Momento Mori (Thanks be to God). Remember you must die).

In 1652, on the death of the eleventh Campbell laird, the lands passed through his daughter to the Livingstons of Glentirran. In 1810, Sir Alexander Livingston died childless, and the lands passed once more through the female line to his maternal grandmother, to the Callanders of Craigforth, who took the name Campbell upon attaining the Ardkinglass Campbell estates.

Kilmorich Church

It was in Sir Alexander's time that construction on Kilmorich Church in Cairndow commenced, being built between 1808 and 1816. Burial of the family moved from Lochgoilhead to Ardkinglass in Cairndow at this time, and the family was thereafter buried at Kilmorich.

Drawing of Kilmorich Church (1848)

On the sale of the estate in 1905, the curator, Niall Diarmid Campbell, later to become the tenth duke of Argyll, wrote letters "to all the native men, vassals, and good tenants dwelling on the lands of Ardkinglass both men and women." He recited a history going back to when "the first laird with his three tall sons settled in the place where in obedience to a predicted omen his hamper strings should snap. His father Sir Colin Campbell, Lord of Lochow did in the year of our Lord 1396 grant to him and his posterity that spot known as Ardkinglass ... for as long as 'woods should grow and waters run' ... on condition he should keep ... two war-galleys, one of eight oars, the other of six to serve the Lord of Lochow and the King of the Scots in times of tumult and war".[3]

The Early Lairds of Ardkinglass

Campbell traced the valiant and sometimes dark history of the lairds. This included how, in 1513, the fourth laird ordered that the Lochgoilhead priest pray all the time for the family, but the laird was slain in 1513 at Flodden Field and borne home by his clan. His chief, the second earl of Argyll, also fell that fateful day, along with the Scots King James IV and much of the Scots nobility.

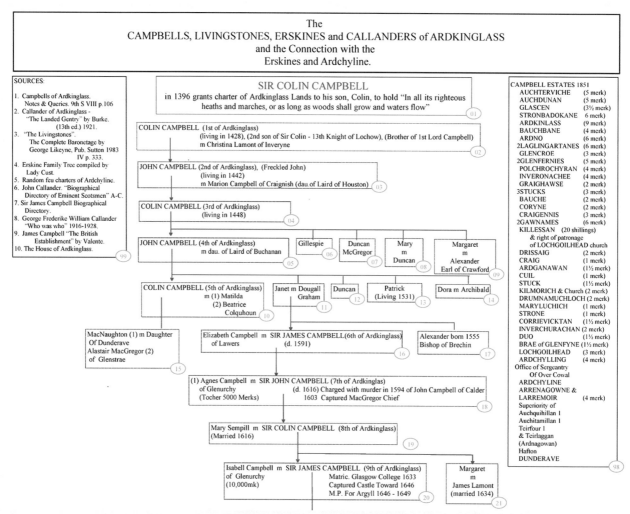

Upper section of a genealogical chart
showing first nine Lairds of Ardkinglass

The fifth laird was rewarded by King James V, who granted him and his descendants the right to claim the crown taxes for the "Assize Herrings" in the Western Seas stretching from the Pentland Firth to the Mull of Galloway, including the Clyde Basin.[4] This was a tax or custom of a thousand herrings levied on each fishing boat employed in the herring industry. It formed part of crown revenues[5].

The fifth laird's nephew, Sir James, the sixth laird, was appointed by James V to the Privy Council and for many years was the king's comptroller. He was appointed tutor and guardian to the seventh earl of Argyll, who was brought up under Sir James's tuition at Ardkinglass.

Yet Sir James's son, Sir John, the seventh laird, had a record "the most ferocious we possess."[6] He was charged with being an accessory to the murder of the laird of Calder. Campbell of Calder was shot through the heart by a man called McKeller with a hackbut supplied by Campbell of Ardkinglass.[7] It seems Calder was another curator of the young seventh earl of Argyll, of whom Ardkinglass was said to be violently jealous. Sir John's trial showed deeds of "incredible malignity and wickedness."[8] He was put on trial on three occasions but not convicted, owing to his disclosures as to the complicity of many others. It is said he sought to regain the earl's affections by magical means—using a warlock minister, Patrick McQueen—without success.[9] In 1615, he went to Islay and Rathlin, where his atrocities included flinging women and children down a precipice. On return, his Ardkinglass galley capsized off Strone of Glen Siora. He drowned, but a vassal named McDougal saved his son, Sir Colin who became the eighth laird.[10]

The ninth laird, Sir James, fought in 1645 during the Civil War at Inverlochy against the Royalist Montrose and survived that defeat, where forty Campbell lairds died. Nine years later, he was indicted for the murder of Sir John Lamont, his brother-in-law, whose clan in Cowal had turned against the Campbells after the Campbell defeat at Inverlochy. In 1662, he was declared a fugitive and traitor and was never restored to his barony. However, his eldest son, Sir Colin, the tenth laird, at the intercession of the ninth earl of Argyll, was reinvested and created a baronet by Charles II. For more than a year, he was compelled to hide in a cave above Moneveckatan in Hell's Glen, near Loch Goil when Ardkinglass Castle was occupied by John Murray, the marquess of Atholl. He supported his chief, the ninth earl of Argyll, in his unsuccessful uprising with the duke of Monmouth against James VII (James II of England). It was said by Lord Macaulay that the marquess was false, fickle and pusillanimous though his grandson Lord George Murray became a notable Jacobite general for Bonny Prince Charlie.

When finally captured in 1685, the year Catholic James VII became king, Sir Colin was imprisoned in Edinburgh Castle. But with the accession of the Protestant King William and Queen Mary, he enjoyed greater tranquillity, becoming a member of Parliament in 1693. He then pursued witches and warlocks, of whom he was assured by the kirk session there was a "notable quantity in the parish."[11] In 1709, he was laid to rest in Lochgoilhead Church.

His son, Sir James, the eleventh laird, was a member of Parliament for thirty-two years. In 1710, he obtained possession of the McNaughton of Dunderave estates, over which he held bonds. This ended eight hundred years of McNaughton possession of those lands.[12] His two sons died young (attributed by some to the curse of a spaewife), so he devised the barony to his daughter, Helen. She married Sir James Livingston, who became the twelfth laird.[13]

The Livingstons

Helen's son, also called Sir James Livingston, became the thirteenth laird. He assumed the name and arms of Ardkinglass and fought on the triumphant Hanoverian side with his Argyll chief against the Jacobites in 1746 at Culloden.

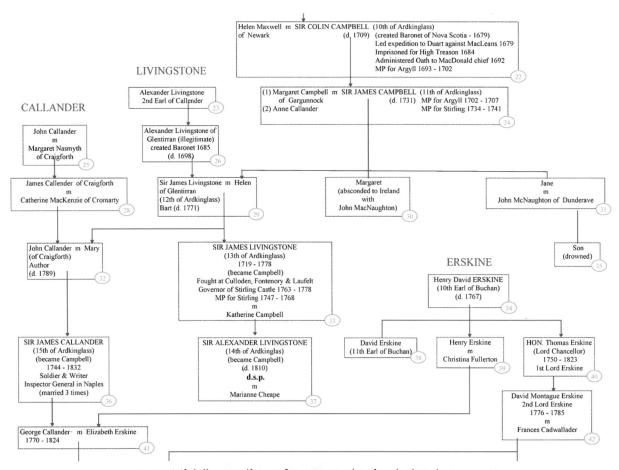

Middle section of a genealogical chart
showing 10th, 11th, 12th, 13th and 14th Lairds of Ardkinglass

Sir James Livingston's son, the fourteenth laird, built a large house at Ardkinglass as well as the church at Kilmorich in Cairndow. Since he had no issue, the baronetcy became extinct, and the estates passed to his cousin, who styled himself wrongly "Sir" James Callander. He was the maternal grandson of Helen, the heiress of Ardkinglass, who had married Sir James Livingston, the twelfth laird.

It is Sir James, who spent nearly all his life abroad owing to his debts which began the great drain on the Estate, to whom Niall Campbell attributed the fall in the fortunes of the family.[14] But as will be shown, the Callanders were blighted with subsequent misfortunes as well.

CHAPTER 2

THE ADVENTURER, JAMES CALLANDER, OF CRAIGFORTH AND ARDKINGLASS

James Callander of Craigforth and Ardkinglass

James Callander, the fifteenth laird, was born at Ardkinglass in 1745, the year of the second Jacobite rebellion. His flamboyant and colourful life is well documented in two volumes of his memoirs.[15] He was the eldest of seventeen children and was married four times. His last bride, in 1815, married him when she was nineteen and he was seventy years old.

Military Background

James Callander fought as a volunteer in the Prussian army in the Seven Years War (1755–1764)[16] under Frederick the Great and under the immediate command of Ferdinand of Brunswick. This war greatly expanded Britain's possessions.

Callander recounts that King George III observed him at military manoeuvres: "If I may be pardoned for the vanity of reporting, the King was pleased to say 'that he had never seen a better looking man, or a better looking horse.'"[17] Later Callander was imprisoned by Napoleon, who he claimed bought a horse from him for 1,200 louis d'ors, but he was only liberated from this imprisonment after the battle of Waterloo in 1815.[18]

Social Life

Callander shot on the estate belonging to the wit Voltaire, whom he thought very conceited[19] and also shot on the estate of Monsieur Fouche,[20] the sinister, revolutionary minister of police. He also dined with the notable French general Prince Conde who commanded at the battle of Johannesberg against Prince of Brunswick for whom James Callander fought.[21]

He joined a London club in Mayfair called "The Pandemonium," where he met the poet Oliver Goldsmith, the lexicographer Doctor Johnson, and the actor David Garrick.[22] Campbell's daughter Caroline, by his third wife, married Thomas Sheridan, son of the playwright and politician Richard Sheridan.[23]

The French Revolution

In 1789 Callander inherited his father's Craigforth Estate.[24] He was attached to the British Embassy in Paris shortly after and was among the last handful of British subjects to leave Paris as King Louis XVI and his wife, Marie Antoinette, were seized by the Parisian mob and hurried to their doom. He found two of the French king's dogs wandering the Paris streets and took them back to the recently inherited Craigforth Estate. One he called "Bastille," after the taking of that prison, and the other "Poissarde," after the celebrated fishwives who had gone to Versailles to bring the king to Paris.[25]

Later Callander went to Naples, where Lord Nelson asked him to go to the Ionian Islands to enlist the inhabitants in their attachment to Britain.[26] He set off for Corfu, then Zante, where he fortified the harbour on Nelson's instructions.[27]

Financial Difficulties

Callander struggled with domestic and financial problems throughout his long life. A debt incurred by James Callander's father to Sir Alexander Livingston, the thirteenth laird, by which James Callander himself was bound, was enforced against James Callander by Sir Alexander's son, the fourteenth laird. Alexander's son had just lost an election by one vote, which he attributed to James Callander voting for his rival. Callander found himself arrested in the streets of Stirling.[28] He recounts that he was obliged to "retire to the continent" on at least two occasions: once following a dual in which his opponent received unspecified injuries,[29] the other occasion on account of debts owed.[30]

Craigforth and Ardkinglass had rentals at that time amounting to £4,000 per annum, but Callander did not inherit Craigforth until 1789 nor Ardkinglass until 1810.[31] He only learnt that he had inherited Ardkinglass in 1813, at which time he was in a French prison and the fourteenth laird had been dead for three years.[32]

*Ardkinglass Castle built by Sir Alexander Campbell (14th Laird)
in place of earlier castle which had 4 turrets.*

After his release from prison in 1815, he married his fourth wife, who was but nineteen years old;[33] however, he was pursued by a French woman who claimed he had earlier married her and that he was therefore a bigamist. The claim was heard in the Scots Courts and went all the way to the House of Lords, where he said he got some vindication.[34] No doubt these misfortunes contributed to the financial woes that Niall Campbell said led to the eventual sale of the Ardkinglass Estate.[35]

Successors

Callander's eldest son, George Callander, married Elizabeth Erskine, who was the daughter of the outstanding Lord Advocate Henry Erskine who is a subject of the next chapter. George Callander moved to set aside his father's entailed right to the Craigforth Estate on account of debts incurred by him against the Estate.[36] However, George Callander predeceased his father, dying in 1824, and on James Callander's death, George Callander's son, James Henry Callander, became the fifteenth laird, whose family are discussed in chapter 4.

CHAPTER 3

THE ERSKINE BROTHERS

Eleventh Earl of Buchan, David Erskine

David Erskine, 11ᵗʰ Earl of Buchan 1742 to 1829 John Brown photographer Antonia Reeve

It was through James Henry Callander's mother, Elizabeth Erskine, who married George Callander, that the Callanders first became linked with the family of the Erskine earls of Buchan. Originally the Erskines were from Renfrewshire, in which both a town and a bridge bear the Erskine name. Elizabeth's father, Henry Erskine, was a younger brother of the earl of Buchan who successfully redeemed the fortunes of the impoverished estate he inherited, though it was Buchan's two younger and more extravagant brothers who became famous.

Buchan was grand master of the Scottish Freemasons from 1782 to 1784 and a patron of the arts. Buchan founded the Society of Antiquarians of Scotland and was elected a member of the American Antiquarians Society, the oldest historical society in that country with a national focus.[37] Buchan supported the Americans in their wars of independence. He considered moving to the United States[38] himself but finally settled at Dryborough Abbey. He corresponded with George Washington, Benjamin Franklin, and Thomas Jefferson.[39] He gave Washington a snuffbox made from an oak tree that had sheltered Sir William Wallace after the battle of Falkirk, and later Washington bequeathed the snuffbox back to Buchan.[40] Perhaps David Erskine's most notable achievement was in regard to the election of Scottish peers in Parliament, which ended the government's practice of sending down for election only those peers the government believed likely to favour the views of the administration.[41]

Henry Erskine

*Henry Erskine, Lord
Advocate, by Raeburn*

Sir Walter Scott described Henry as "the most good natured man he ever knew,"[42] despite Scott being a Tory and Henry Erskine a Whig, at a time of particularly acrimonious party politics. Henry Erskine became dean of the Faculty of Advocates, in which he championed the independence of the Scottish Bar from political influence in opposing the government's treason and sedition bills. In doing so, he was compelled to stand down as dean. He later became lord advocate in the Whig administration. He defended Deacon Brodie, the celebrated thief who was a town councillor, about whom Robert Louis Stevenson wrote a play (and later *Dr Jekyll and Mr Hyde*). When Deacon Brodie was under sentence of death, he believed that he would be resuscitated after his hanging by a quack French doctor.[43]

Henry was a man of many brilliant gifts. Not only was he endowed with a handsome presence, a fascinating manner, and a sparkling wit, but he was regarded as the most eloquent speaker by far at the Scottish Bar in his time. Lord Brougham said, "if I were to name the most consummate exhibition of forensic talent that I ever witnessed whether in the skilful conduct of the argument, the felicity of the copious illustrations, the cogency of the reasoning or the dexterous appeal to the prejudices of the court, I should without hesitation at once point to his address in Maitland's case."[44]

Another distinguished lawyer, Lord Cockburn, said that "nothing was so sour as not to be sweetened by the glance, the voice, the gaiety, and the beauty of Henry Erskine."[45] In his early days, he was one of the most persevering of wags. It was his especial delight to tease Sir James Colquhoun of Luss, who was the principal clerk of sessions. He amused himself by making faces at Sir James as he sat at the clerks table beneath the judges. At last Sir James could stand it no longer and disturbed the gravity of the court by rising and exclaiming "my Lord – my Lord – I wish you would speak to Henry; he's aye making faces at me." Henry was looking graver than the judges, however, when this was said. But when Sir James looked again, he was met by a new grimace from his tormentor and once more convulsed the bench, bar, and audience by roaring out in his rage, "See there, my Lord! He's at it again."[46]

Lord Cockburn spoke of this "tall and rather slender figure, a face sparkling with vivacity, a clear sweet voice, and a general appearance of elegance, which gave him a striking and pleasing appearance."[47] But perhaps there is no better testimony to his worth than the inscription on the tablet fixed to his birth place: "No poor man wanted a friend while Harry Erskine lived."[48]

Thomas Erskine

Thomas Erskine, Lord Chancellor, by Sir T Lawrence

Despite the accolades of the first two brothers, it was the youngest brother, Thomas Erskine, who became the most eminent of the three. Thomas rose to become head of the Judiciary as lord chancellor in the Whig ministry "of all the talents" led by Charles Fox. However, it was not as lord chancellor he was to be remembered, but as Britain's leading advocate. To this day he is regarded by most lawyers as the greatest advocate the English Bar has ever produced.[49] The law Lord, Patrick Devlin, said of him "I believe most of the well informed would agree upon him (Erskine) than any other as the greatest advocate who ever practiced at the English Bar".[50]

Lord Campbell, who later became lord chancellor himself, was a younger contemporary and said of Thomas Erskine: "He displayed genius united with public principle; he saved the liberties of his country; he was the brightest ornament of which the English Bar can boast; and from his vivacity, his courtesy, and his kindness of heart he was the charm of every society which he entered."[51]

At fourteen years, much against his will, Thomas Erskine was sent to sea as a midshipman. The Erskine family had been impoverished earlier in the Jacobite cause and lost their Renfrewshire lands. On his return from voyages, he was called to the Bar in 1778 and made good use of his naval knowledge in his first case, in which he represented a Captain Baillie. Captain Baillie faced a charge of criminal libel in consequence of his exposing abuses in the management of Greenwich Hospital by the first lord of the admiralty, Lord Sandwich.

The young barrister, who knew that Lord Sandwich was the real instigator of the proceedings, made a fierce attack on him. When he mentioned the name of Sandwich, the Chief Justic Lord Mansfield interrupted him and reminded him that the nobleman was not before the court. Erskine however, proceeded:

> "I know that he is not formally before the court; but for that very reason I will bring him before the court. He has placed these men in the front of the battle, in hopes to escape under their shelter; but I will not join in battle with them; their vices, through screwed up to the highest pitch of human depravity, are not of dignity enough to vindicate the combat with me. I will drag him to light who is the dark mover behind the scene of iniquity. I assert that the Earl of Sandwich has but one road to escape out of this business without pollution and disgrace; and that is, by publicly disavowing the acts of the prosecutors, and restoring Captain Baillie to his command. If he does this, then his offence will be no more than the too common one of having suffered his own personal interests to prevail over his public duty, in placing his voters in the hospital. But if, on the contrary, he continues to protect the prosecutors, in spite of the evidence of their guilt, which has excited the abhorrence of the numerous audience that crowd this court; if he keeps this injured man suspended, or dares to turn that suspension into a removal, I shall then not scruple to declare him an accomplice in their guilt, a shameless oppressor, a disgrace to his rank and traitor to his trust".[52]

Erskine's advocacy was so vehement that Chief Justice Mansfield several times exhorted him to moderate his language, but Erskine did not abate his vehemence. Later, when asked how he had the courage to speak up as he did, he replied that he thought his little children were plucking his robe and that he heard them saying, "Now, father, is the time to get us bread." The rule against Captain Baillie was discharged.

This case was followed by his successful defence of Lord George Gordon, on a charge of high treason and Erskine's carriage was pulled by the London mob through the streets of London. Gordon had proceeded at the head of 40,000 people to the House of Commons to present a petition for repeal of some concessions to Catholics. In the course of the procession, there had been fatalities and Gordon was indicted. Within five years, Erskine had been made a Queens Counsel.

In 1784 he appeared in the case of the Dean of Asaph who was prosecuted for circulating a tract in Welsh, pointing out some of the defects in the existing constitution of Parliament. The case was tried before Mr Justice Buller (an ancestor of a later Law Lord Viscount Dilhorne). At that time it was for judges to decide whether a document was a criminal libel or not, and the jury could decide only the question of "publication" of the alleged libel which was ordinarily a formality. The Whigs much disliked this legal doctrine because it deprived juries of an important part of their function, and placed the right of free speech under the control of the judges. At the trial of the Dean of Asaph for libel, Erskine contended that the jury, and not the judge, should decide the question of libel or no libel but Mr Justice Buller, taking the then prevailing judicial view, directed that the jury was merely to find the fact of publication and the truth of the innuendo as laid, and stated that it was for the judge to decide whether or not the words constituted a libel. The jury, however, yielding to the influence of Erskine's reasoning, found the Dean "guilty of publishing only". The judge took exception to the word "only", but Erskine demanded that it should stand as part of the verdict. The altercation went thus:

Buller:	You say he is guilty of publishing the pamphlet, and that the meaning of the innuendoes is as stated in the indictment?
A Juror:	Certainly.
Erskine:	Is the word "only" to stand as part of your verdict?
A Juror:	Certainly.
Erskine:	Then I insist it shall be recorded.
Buller:	Then the verdict must be misunderstood. Let me understand the jury.
Erskine:	The jury do understand their verdict.
Buller:	Sir, I will not be interrupted.
Erskine:	I stand here as an advocate for a brother citizen, and I desire that the word "only" may be recorded.
Buller:	Sit down, Sir. Remember your duty, or I shall be obliged to proceed in another manner.
Erskine:	Your Lordship may proceed in what manner you think fit. I know my duty as well as your Lordship knows yours. I shall not alter my conduct.

The jury were asked again by the Judge to withdraw, and they finally brought in the verdict, "guilty of publishing, but whether a libel or not we do not find".[53]

The legal question in the dispute was ultimately set to rest in 1792 by the passing of the Libel Act, which enacted that the question of libel or no libel in each case was one for the jury.

Eloquence

Thomas Erskine was also successful in the defence of a publisher named Stockdale who had published a condemnation by an author called Logan of the impeachment of the Indian governor Warren Hastings. Erskine's oration in Stockdale's case was described by Lord Campbell as "the finest passage to be found in ancient or modern oratory, for imagery, for passion, for pathos, for variety and beauty of cadence, for the concealment of art, for effect in gaining the object of the orator."[54]

Hastings had been impeached by Parliament, instigated by the Whig leaders, and Logan protested in his pamphlet against the wave of obloquy that was poured on Hastings as a result of his impeachment. He maintained that the impeachment was carried on for motives of personal animosity and not from regard for public justice. Charles Fox, a close political ally of Erskine, brought this publication before the House of Commons, contending it was a libel on the managers of the impeachment and prayed that the attorney general might prosecute Stockdale as the publisher.

Erskine wished to engage sympathy for Hastings so as to justify the author Logan's defence of him. However, he had to defend Hastings cautiously so as not to bring upon the author any of the odium of the charges against Hastings nor to make the defence of the book dependent on proving the innocence of Hastings. He opened by remarking that people might wonder at the absence of accusers from India, and then Erskine moved to the content of the book:

> For although I am neither his (Mr Hastings) counsel, nor desire to have anything to do with his guilt or innocence, yet in the collateral defence of my client, I am driven to state matter which may be considered by many as hostile to the impeachment; for if our dependencies have been secured and their interests promoted, I am driven, in the defence of my client, to remark, that it is mad and preposterous to bring to the standard of justice and humanity the exercise of a dominion founded upon violence and terror. It may and must be true that Mr Hastings has repeatedly offended against the rights and privileges of Asiatic government, if he was the faithful deputy of a power which could not maintain itself for an hour without trampling upon both: he may and must have offended against the laws of God and nature, if he was the faithful viceroy of an empire wrested in blood from the people to whom God and nature had given it: he may and must have preserved that unjust dominion over timorous and abject nations by a terrifying, overbearing, insulting superiority, if he was the faithful administrator of your Government, which having no root in consent or affection, no foundation in similarity of interests, nor support from any one principle which cements men together in society, could only be upheld by alternate stratagem and force … I know what they feel, and how such feelings can alone be repressed. I have heard them, in my youth, from a naked savage, in the indignant character of a prince surrounded by his subjects, addressing the governor of a British colony, holding a bundle of sticks in his hand as the notes of his unlettered eloquence. "Who is it?" said the jealous ruler over the desert encroached upon by the restless foot of English adventure, "Who is it that causes this river to rise in the high mountains, and to empty itself into the ocean? Who is it that causes to blow the loud winds of winter, and that calms them again in the summer? Who is it that rears up the shade of those lofty forests, and blasts them with the quick lightening at his pleasure? The same Being who gave to you a country on the other side of the waters, and gave ours to us; and by this title we will defend it," said the warrior, throwing down his tomahawk upon the ground,

and raising the war-sound of his nation. These are the feelings of subjugated man all around the globe; and depend upon it, nothing but fear will control where it is vain to look for affection.[55]

Erskine also defended Hadfield, charged with treason for shooting at George III in Drury Lane Theatre and obtained a verdict of not guilty by reason of insanity. Furthermore, his reasoning in relation to the law of insanity has been adopted by judges ever since.

He defended many political reformers with success, such as Thomas Hardy and Horne Tooke, charged with high treason by a nervous government afraid that any reform to the parliamentary system would usher in a revolution similar to the one in France with its guillotining of the French king. His defences included that of Thomas Paine, the author of the "Rights of Man."

Erskine showed fearlessness in opposing injustice where perpetrated by government ministers, as in Captain Baillie's case; in combating the crown prosecutors in Gordon's case; and in challenging oppressive laws such as that which defined high treason in terms far too wide. He never sought to ingratiate himself with the powerful or even with his own political allies, such as Charles Fox. Indeed, he offended George IV by representing Thomas Paine, and later in championing the cause of his estranged wife, Queen Caroline.

On becoming lord chancellor, he took as his motto "trial by jury." His advocacy for the independence of the jury from political influence, for the freedom of the press, and for the preservation of the rule of law did much to prevent violent revolution in Scotland and England.

Comparison of the Three Brothers

Sir Walter Scott wrote of the three brothers "that the two celebrated lawyers were not more gifted by nature than, I think, (Buchan) was but restraints of a profession kept eccentricity of the family in order. Henry Erskine was the best natured man I ever knew ... both Henry and Thomas were saving men, yet both died very poor. [Thomas] at one time possessed £200,000; [Henry] a considerable fortune. The Earl alone has died wealthy (through saving). It is saving, not getting, that is the mother of riches. They all had wit. The earl was crackbrained and caustic, Henry's was of the very kindest, best humoured and gayest that ever cheered society, that of Lord Erskine was moody and maddish. But I never saw him in his best days."[56]

It was true that Buchan had a large conceit of himself, to which Scott demonstrated an aversion. Thomas he scarcely knew, as he himself recognised, since so much of Thomas's life was spent outside of Scotland, but Henry he knew well.

It was said of Buchan that he had an excessive vanity and egotism. However, as Lieutenant Colonel Erskine points out, "One might think that with an intensely vain man like Lord Buchan nothing would have gone down so well as flattery, but not so; there was with him a just middle line which might not be overstepped. This fact had hardly been sufficiently realised by Robert Burns. More than one letter of the poet to Lord Buchan has been preserved in which the poet meant to be only complimentary, but which the Earl thought too strong and the Earl made a quaint endorsement of it with the comment 'Swift says praise is like ambergris; a little is odorous – much stinks.'"[57]

As Lieutenant Colonel Erskine said in his biography of Henry, if "the independence of the Scottish Bar" was an appropriate phrase in connection with Henry Erskine's career—or "trial by jury" with that of the younger brother—then "the independence of the Scottish peerage" seems to be a motto not undeserved by the Earl of Buchan.[58]

CHAPTER 4
THE TRAGIC FAMILY OF JAMES HENRY CALLANDER

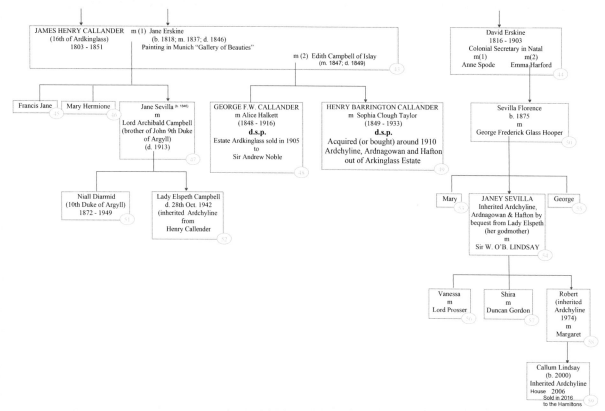

*Lower section of a genealogical chart
showing from James Henry Callander to the present day.*

The story of James Henry Callander's family is a sombre and tragic one. His first wife, Janey Erskine, was the granddaughter of the great advocate Thomas Erskine, and his mother was the daughter of Thomas's brother Henry Erskine, making them second cousins. Janey Erskine was the daughter of David Erskine, the British envoy in Munich, and she was painted there at nineteen for the King Ludwig I of Bavaria's "Gallery of Beauties." The same year she married but was dead by twenty-eight, having given birth to three girls.

James Henry Callander's second marriage, which occurred the year after her death, was also short-lived. He married the nineteen-year-old Edith Campbell of Islay, and she was dead by twenty-two, leaving two boys: George and Henry Callander, aged two and one dying the same year she gave birth to Henry. Two years after her death in 1849, James Henry Callander was himself dead, and so all five children were now orphaned.

*Lady Jane Erskine,
as painted for King Ludwig I of
Bavaria's "Gallery of Beauties".*

*Janey Sevilla Callander
(mother of Lady Elspeth)*

Four of the five orphaned children did not have children themselves, leaving only the third daughter of the first marriage, Janey Sevilla, to continue the line.

Janey Sevilla Callander

Janey Sevilla Callander's mother, Janey Erskine, died shortly after giving birth to her, and Janey Sevilla was only five when her father died. Janey Sevilla was made a ward of the eighth duke of Argyll and brought up at Inveraray Castle, where she met and married the eighth duke's second son, Lord Archibald Campbell. She was described by Oscar Wilde as "the moon lady" for her beautiful beryl eyes.

The eldest son of the eighth duke, John, married Princess Louise, the fourth daughter of Queen Victoria and the first of her children to marry a commoner. Princess Louise had no children herself and therefore gave special attention to the two children of Janey Sevilla, Niall and Elspeth Campbell. The lives of these children are discussed in the next chapters. Neither Niall nor Elspeth married. It is possible that this decision was, at least partly, influenced by the fear that the laws of consanguinity warned against the wisdom of doing so. Their Erskine grandmother, Janey Erskine, had married her cousin James Henry Callander.

George and Henry Callander

George Callander, seventeenth and last Callander Laird of Ardkinglass

Henry Callander at Port Henry, below Ardchyline House, St Catherine's, which he had built in circa. 1910

The two boys by James Henry Callander's second marriage, George and Henry Callander, both married but had no children. George became the last Campbell/Callander laird (the seventeenth) before the Ardkinglass Estates, burdened with debt, had to be sold in 1905 to Sir Andrew Noble.

Ardchyline, Arinagowan, and Halftown

Since the sale of the Ardkinglass Estate would deprive Henry Callander of his inheritance, he was allowed to buy a small part of the estate, comprising Ardchyline, Arinagowan, and Halftown out of the estate sale on payment of £6,000. Having done so, he had Ardchyline House built in 1910 by Archibald Ferguson in Strachur. He spent most of his life in the navy, and his naval aide built a boathouse and harbour directly opposite Inveraray Castle across Loch Fyne, which is called "Port Henry." He would then motor across the loch to see his nephew and niece, Niall and Elspeth Campbell, at Inveraray Castle, where Niall had become the tenth duke of Argyll in 1914.

George spent much of his adult life in a mental asylum. At George's funeral on a rainy day in 1916, Henry said, "Even the heavens weep for my brother's wasted life."

Gravestones at Kilmorich,
showing James Henry Callander, his wives Jane Erskine and Charlotte (Edith) Campbell,
and daughter Janey Callander.

When Henry Callander died childless in 1933, he was buried at Kilmorich Church, where his parents and half-sister Janey Sevilla, whose gravestones are set against the church wall, were also laid to rest. Since Niall had now become duke of Argyll, Henry's estate of Ardchyline, Arinagowan, and Halftown was assigned to his sister, Lady Elspeth Campbell.

The Current Dukedom of Argyll

Duke Niall's death without children in 1949 meant that the dukedom now passed to the grandson of the eighth duke's third son, Lord Walter Campbell, who was named Ian Douglas. He became the eleventh duke, and his eldest son, also Ian, became the twelfth duke who became the father of Torquil, the present duke of Argyll.

CHAPTER 5

LADY ELSPETH CAMPBELL: THE FAIRY GODMOTHER

Lady Elspeth playing with a dog

Elspeth Campbell, sister of the tenth duke of Argyll, was a remarkable highlander. Born in London on November 2, 1873, she was brought up at Kensington Palace and Inveraray Castle, in Argyll, the home of her grandparents, the eighth duke and duchess of Argyll. When the eighth duke died, the castle became the home of her uncle, now Duke John Campbell, and his wife, Princess Louise, the fourth daughter of Queen Victoria. Elspeth's father, Lord Archibald Campbell, was John's younger brother. The princess was childless, so she took a very close interest in her husband's family and, in particular, in Elspeth and her brother, Niall.

From an early age, Elspeth made an unforgettable impression upon those she met.

Mr Gladstone, the former Prime Minister, was one of the young lady's most ardent admirers. The ex-premier is said to have declared that "Ms Campbell's features may be traced to a revival of 'the old Irish beauty' about which our forefathers were wont to rave."[59]

Elspeth's First Season

Elspeth was known as Niky. In Jehanne Wake's book *Princess Louise,* the excited preparation for the first season is thus conveyed:

> The family, that is Niky's Aunts, Princess Louise and Molly Dawkins, had decided that Elspeth's mother Janey, for all her charm and beauty, was far too "eccentric and cranky" to be relied upon to arrange her daughter's first season.

The Princess taught Niky how to walk into a room gracefully and to cerclè as she had been taught all those years ago at Osborne and Windsor; Brother Niall was ordered up from Oxford to act as her partner; dressmakers and hairdressers were consulted so that Niky had some pretty frocks and large, picture hats. The family tomboy was well on the way to becoming a poised, beautiful young lady.

Lady Elspeth Campbell coming out

On the afternoon of May 10, 1894, a box of a house in Hill Street received a great many visitors. They called to see a young debutante in her presentation frock and her aunt Molly Dawkins admitted that "dearly as I love her I never before realised how beautiful she is." Niky was faultlessly dressed, her curly, almost black hair, beautifully done, her lovely aquamarine and diamonds, "exactly matched her eyes," yet, in her manner, she was "as calm and natural as if she was with her guinea pigs."

At her first ball at the duchess of Abercorns, on 23 May 1894, Niky made "a tremendous sensation." The prime minister, Arthur Balfour, stood silent and then said, "That is not a girl, that is an angel."[60]

23

Her Admirers

Lady Elspeth Campbell swathed in the Campbell Tartan

In April 1897, Ellen Terry, the Shakespearean actress, recalled that Princess Louise had brought Elspeth "looking lovely" to see her play.[61]

In 1903, A. E. W. Mason dedicated his book *The Four Feathers* to Elspeth, and it became so popular that it was made into a film several times.

A pipe march, "Miss Elspeth Campbell," was named after her.

Elspeth was a friend of the fairy story writer Andrew Lang, who dedicated several works to her: his poem on Culloden; his book *Prince Charles Edward Stuart*, published in 1903; and the *Blue Fairy Book*. In a poem dedicated to her, he said, "The little girl in the poem had many friends in fairyland, as well as pets among the wood folk. And she has grown up among the books year by year, sometimes writing stories herself of the birds and beasts she had attained, being throughout her life the dearest friend of a man who crowned the Christmas books 25 years ago."

The Wee Folk

Both Elspeth and her brother, Niall, believed in the "wee folk." "These are usually little green things that peer at you from behind trees, as squirrels do, and disappear into the earth. The Duke had visited numerous fairy haunts. So had his sister, Lady Elspeth (Campbell), who at dinner one night announced with serenity 'the fairies are out in their sieves tonight'. Her brother replied 'crossing over to Ireland, no doubt' and he reflected 'we are not good enough for them in Scotland. Why! Last year at Tipperary, there were so many of the them that they caused a traffic block'."[62]

Highland Upbringing

From an early age, Elspeth had been brought up in the highland way. She played the bagpipes and the harp; she collected and wrote short stories about highland tales and mysteries.[63] She was to become president of the local Inveraray branch of the Gaelic Society, and she often sang or accompanied singers of Gaelic songs on the piano. She shared with her brother an astonishing historical knowledge of the Campbell family and could recite, on both sides of the family, Campbell ancestors for many generations. Like her brother she could usually identify not only the place and hour of birth of an ancestor, but frequently the minute as well. She was well read, and she and her brother usually managed the *Times* crossword before breakfast.[64]

The Phantom Galley

Elspeth's father was Lord Archibald Campbell, the ninth duke's brother, who died in 1913 at Rhudnacraig on the shores of Loch Fyne near Inveraray. At the time of his death, Elspeth's mother, Janey Sevilla Callender, heard beautiful music and saw a galley in the sky. Jehanne Wake described it thus:

> In the London papers there had been talk of a strange German airship floating over Loch Fyne … (the family) knew better. It was, of course, the phantom Galley of Lorne, which always appears when a Chief, or one closely connected with him such as Lord Archie, passed from his people. Elspeth's brother, Niall, said that the phantom galley had been seen everywhere and that it was "filled with glittering figures … and is managed by the very early generations of the Clan, right back in the Celtic ages who did it regularly as a compliment."
>
> The galley floated over Inveraray before sailing towards Inischonain, the former Campbell headquarters on Loch Awe.[65]

Despite great beauty and intellect, Elspeth Campbell never married. Her name was linked with a number of aristocrats, including one of the Percy Family in Northumberland; Sir Norman Lamont, whose estates were on the south side of Loch Fyne; and a third unknown person who it was thought died in the Boer War. However, there is no firm evidence that she was ever formally engaged.

Inveraray Home

In 1914, her brother, Niall, became the tenth duke of Argyll on the death of his uncle, and Elspeth moved into Rhundacraig, which had been her father's home until his death. There she remained until the house was requisitioned in the Second World War, when she moved to Inveraray Castle to live with her brother. Since her brother did not marry either, Elspeth played hostess at the castle to visitors.

She was a keen fisher, and on occasion the duke would say to her at breakfast, "Elspeth, we need fish for our guests." The next day she would miraculously produce two salmon. She made her own flies and on Sundays was often seen in church eying the ostrich hats of the ladies. After the service, she would ask them to provide a feather from their Sunday hat.

During World War I, she organised the despatch of goods to the Argyll regiment. She took a close interest in the Inveraray Parish, funding the services of both a district nurse and the parish minister. Unlike her Episcopalian brother, Elspeth was a devout Presbyterian, and her condition for supporting the Presbyterian Church was that the minister had to be a Gaelic speaker.

Visits to Dalchenna

It was on account of my mother's family, who were Erskines on her mother's side, that I came to explore the connection between the Erskines and the Argyll Campbells.

Between the two World Wars my mother's family frequently visited Dalchenna, near Inveraray, for the grouse shooting in September. My mother was Elspeth's goddaughter, and remembers her as a formidable presence at Inveraray Castle, swathed in Campbell tartan. But my mother shared with Elspeth a belief in the "wee folk." Indeed Niall and Elspeth would frequently talk to their unseen friends, and food was often left out for the fairies at night.

Elspeth's Death

In October 1942 Elspeth died. She had not been in good health since she had suffered a fall from a boulder on the River Aray whilst fishing. During Elspeth's last illness, a pair of robins, which she called Mr and Mrs Oliver, fluttered outside her window at the castle. Elspeth had a remarkable affinity with birds and other creatures. Every now and then, Mr Oliver flew into Elspeth's room and laid a worm on her pillow. But it was to no avail. Her funeral service took place at Kilmalieu Cemetery near Inveraray itself. As her coffin was conveyed to the cemetery, observers noticed that the noisy seagulls who wheel around Inveraray Pier had fallen silent and stood on the seafront like sentinels at the passing of a great figure.

My mother received the news of Elspeth's death in Dorset, where she was managing a farm. Then, to her amazement, a notification came from the solicitors that Elspeth had bequeathed to her the Ardchyline Estate. This comprised a sheep farm of 2000 acres; the Edwardian manor house of Ardchyline, built for Henry Callander; Port Henry; three miles of loch frontage between St Catherine's and Strachur on the South side of Loch Fyne; and many personal effects. Neil Munro, in his first novel, *John Splendid*, refers to the deer crossing the ice of Loch Fyne to reach "the oak woods of Ardchyline.[66]" The land also included two old settlements: Arinagowan (Ardnagowan), which once had a village, and Halftown.

Ardchyline House, St Catherine's, Loch Fyne

Amongst my mother's legacy from Elspeth were diamond necklaces, highland broaches (one with "Niky" inscribed) fur coats, old medallions, and clothing made by Elspeth herself with small breast pockets from which the chaffinches and robins could feed.

The inheritance was quite unexpected, and my mother always attributed the favour shown to her to the fact that she shared her godmother's belief in fairies and not any family connection although both had Erskine ancestry on the mother's side.

Halftown Hamlet

Amongst the legacy left by Elspeth was the small hamlet of Halftown, upon which two semi-derelict cottages stood, which are now renovated. This was a highland clachan in the seventeenth and eighteenth centuries, comprising several houses where a blind tailor once lived. The Inveraray writer, Neil Munro, successor to Robert Louis Stevenson, whose writing is perhaps more intrinsically "Highland" than either Stevenson or Sir Walter Scott who were not themselves brought up as he was in Gaelic ways, wrote a famous short story about a Halftown clachan called "The Lost Pibroch." The story tells of a blind tailor who played the "Lost Pibroch" with the consequence, so symbolic of highland life, of inspiring those who heard the pibroch to abandon the hills to make their fortune in other countries, intending to return but never doing so.[67] The cottages, which sit upon the old highland township, have now been refurbished for holiday lets, but their outer walls remain as they were when first built over three hundred years ago.

Halftown Cottages, St Catherine's, Loch Fyne (Leth-Baile in Gaelic)

The Gaelic poet Evan MacColl of Kenmore across Loch Fyne, wrote a love poem called "The Rose of Halftown"—believed to be about Rose Forbes who once lived there and for whom he pined:

Oh it's a pity that me and my love
are not together on the Brae;
driving cattle and the deer
in the shade of the bushes
I would play for her my little song
and pick for her sweet berries
and we'd spend our life
in happiness and plenty[68]

Evan MacColl had a thirst for legendary lore and Gaelic poetry. When not farming or assisting in the herring fishing during the season on Loch Fyne he composed poems about the hills. He was later appointed to a clerkship in Liverpool and later still migrated to Canada.[69]

Niall Campbell outlived Elspeth by seven years. After her death the duke forbade her room at Inveraray Castle to be touched. As to Lady Elspeth, her grave is a simple flat stone in Kilmalieu, only a few metres from that of the great Inveraray writer, Neil Munro. On the stone is the Campbell motto, "Ne Obliviscaris."

CHAPTER 6

NIALL CAMPBELL (THE TENTH DUKE OF ARGYLL)

Niall David Campbell 10th Duke of Argyll as a boy

Niall was born a year before his sister, Elspeth, and outlived her by seven years. Like her, he was deeply immersed in highland ways. From an early age, he carried important administrative duties as curator for the Ardkinglass Estate and, as seen, managed the sale of that estate in 1905 to Sir Andrew Noble when he also wrote the letters to the tenantry about the Ardkinglass lairds.

St Catherine's

Niall lived at Upper Kilcatrine in St Catherine's before becoming duke of Argyll. To the west side of Upper Kilcatrine were the remains of the original "kil" or chapel.[70] The outline of the walls of the medieval chapel, 40 feet by 15 feet, is still discernible. Whilst at Kilcatrine he recounted in his diary on 21 August 1913, a meeting with the great seer, Captain Saddell. He recorded his visions of the "kil" or chapel, from which the name of Kilcatrine, and therefore St Catherine's, derived. First, Niall recounts how the seer precisely and correctly described the physical appearance of the Upper Kilcatrine house builder, Doctor Paterson, and then saw him following Niall and the seer to the "kil" (chapel or cell) to the side of the house. The seer described how the chapel was founded "by Duncan, Lord of Lochow in 1450 (he says it should be 1420) and all the vassals bringing creels of stones from the hill, two or three people in long white robes, probably the monks who served it. He saw the position of all the long vanished windows, the door etc. The passing of the centuries and its slow decay and the falling in of the roof and ruins pulling part of the walls down for other uses." Captain Saddel told Niall how he had seen "hundreds of green fairies dancing on the high road near his own home."[71]

Port Henry

Niall records that the seer met his uncle Henry Callander near the Port Henry boathouse at Ardchyline and Henry appeared covered in seaweed. On the quay was a water maiden combing her hair, "which means he [Henry] will get drowned some day." This prognosis was proved mistaken. Although Henry was a sailor by occupation, he did not later die by drowning.

The Harper at Inveraray Castle

Niall's copious correspondence included learned ecclesiastical debates with local ministers and historical research, such as that supplied to Sir Iain Moncrieffe for his fine book on the highland clans.[72] Both he and Elspeth supplied *Lord Halifax's Ghost Book*[73] with their ghostly experiences at Inveraray Castle. The "elect" guests with adequate psychic powers to experience the supernatural heard the banging of books. According to Niall and Elspeth, this noise was the ghost of the harper who was hanged at Inveraray by Montrose's men during the Civil War.

The New Road Round Loch Fyne

Niall thought nothing of walking the sixteen miles from St Catherine's to Inveraray. He approved of the new road built in 1934, described in a letter to his cousin, Florence Sevilla Glass Hooper (my Erskine grandmother) about the work done on the stretch of road between Cairndow and the Fyne bridge, which then stretched up to "the Rest and Be Thankful."

Sevilla Erskine (Glasshooper) as a child

The Loch Ness Monster

In the same letter Niall gave Cousin Sevilla his views on the Loch Ness monster:

> There is great excitement over this mysterious animal in Loch Ness and we hear the Inverness hotels have never had such crowds in the winter.

> It is certainly not a seal and seems to be some enormous creature like a newt with hummocks on its back – in fact I think there must be several of them, especially if they have always been in that loch as they must have bred. I do not believe a marine creature could get up the River Ness which is usually very shallow. Loch Ness is 750 feet deep whilst Loch Morar is 400 feet more being the seventh deepest in all Europe.[74]

The Second World War

On the 31 August 1939, Niall wrote to his cousin again about the early developments in the war, predicting that Hitler would overreach himself concerning Russia and reprimanding her for not attending Mass.

He wrote:

> I have many letters today as yesterday full of strange bits of news which indicate how touch and go the whole position is. That Hitler has overreached himself over Russia is quite certain though he may not see it for the moment. Ewen Cameron has just rushed in having heard the servants wireless on the backstairs as to the war having begun all along the Corridor and bombing of Cracow.

> Ewen, Cameron and I visited the Lloyds at Minard yesterday and heard ominous news as to child evacuation from my quarry manager at Furnace and the previous day I got at last to see that huge new bridge at Cladich – 200 men are at work on that 4 mile of road and I was astonished at the progress made since June.

> I went to the east turret where any light would be specially visible from the air and the shutters so stiff from long disuse that we could not close them.

> You were lazy not coming in to church when at Cairndow and only going to Dalchena. At such a time everyone ought to hear Mass on a Saturday – a good example to the populace![75]

Then on the 9 November 1939, he wrote to Florence Sevilla:

> If there are excitements on the east coast, there have been plenty on the Clyde. Rosneath was taken over from Aunt L (Princess Louise) by the Balloon people and

convoys of heavy guns put all about for the fleet and then the ships all suddenly left. A whale got into the boom net the other day and set off all the automatic flares and the sirens etc all went off! Enemy planes were twice over the Gareloch etc at 30,000 feet and one of them is the one got down at Dalkeith its pilot only 17. His brother having turned anti-Nazi was shot and the young one was told if he did not fly it he would also be shot.

Today I hear at Rosyth a German bomb fell in the scuppers of the Mohawk – a seaman picked it up and threw it into the sea, it never exploded and proved to be a dud. Sabotage done in the Skoda works where it was made.

On Martin mass (Saturday) we shall have another requiem here.[76]

The Bell Tower

11 August 1931

Inveraray Castle,
Argyll.

My dear Sevilla,

Are you and George going to come up & pay us a visit sometime in August or Sept or October. We should be delighted. I was sorry not to have managed to see you when in the south. I was in London till a few days ago but went down to Brighton for a week over Bank Holiday to get rid of a cold in the head and to watch the incredible crowds sun bathing etc – a most weird sight. Elspeth came to me yesterday from her own house. & has been fishing a lot. It has been lovely weather since I came and much warmer than in the South. We have got in the inside floors of the Belfry and the Roof is finished. At present 2 large steel beams have to be got up through the trap doors of a ton each which are to be the supports for the Bell frame. They tell me that they hope to have everything ready to hoist the Bells up in October so at present they are lying dismantled on the floor of the temporary Shed east of the Church so their voices will not be heard this autumn till they are raised up. Everything so far

*Letter from Niall to Sevilla, including
a reference to the Bell Tower*

The Campbells suffered grievous losses in the First World War. Among those was Niall's cousin Ivar, and he resolved, as honorary colonel of the Eighth Battalion of the Argyle and Sutherland Highlanders, that there should be a memorial to the Campbell dead.[77] As said earlier, Niall was a devout High Church Episcopalian, and it was his ambition for his memorial bell tower to join up with the Episcopalian church where he worshipped.[78] He vigorously pursued donations from clan members and other donors to raise the £21,000 necessary for the tower.

He writes in January 1931 of the progress, specifically of the seven windows being placed and having about £6,000 of the £8,000 secured in donations. He was trying to get the clan in Canada to extinguish the debt.[79]

The oak for the floor and roof had come from Ayr over "the Rest and Be Thankful" by Whit Tuesday of 1931 and the transporters "were much alarmed as they had never been into this district before."[80] The ten bells, cast by a

Loughborough firm, are said to be the second heaviest peel of bells in the world. Several attempts were needed before a lorry finally got the bells to the top of "the Rest and Be Thankful."

By May 1931 the exterior walls, roof, and internal floors were put in and only £1,700 needed for completion.[81] By the 12 September 1931, all ten bells had been safely hoisted and settled on their frames by the foundry workers from Loughborough.

Inveraray and the Bell Tower, across Loch Fyne from St Catherine's.

Niall explains it took nine men to roll the four big bells out of the shed and into the tower, but they were then hoisted in half an hour. The tongues were put in and the chiming hammers adjusted. The bells were then tested and could be heard 30 to 40 miles down the Loch.[82] Each of the ten bells, named after a Celtic saint, were tuned to harmonise with the others.

By the 27 September 1932, the debt for the tower had reduced to £320. Daily boats and buses for the Glasgow holidays arrived, and many climbed the tower. The duke said he strummed tunes to them.[83]

On the 27 May 1933, he reports that a hundred people went up the tower on the previous Monday to gape at the views, and they had paid sixpence a head.[84]

George V died in December 1936. In the spring of 1937, Duke Niall arranged for ten ringers from Paisley to rehearse for the afternoon of Coronation Day for Edward VIII.[85] He and Provost Alex Macintyre had received copper plate invitations to attend,[86] but the coronation of Edward VIII was never to occur. He had formally abdicated by December, and instead it was his brother, Bertie, who was to become George VI on 12 May 1937.

His Burial

In 1949 Niall went to burial with his Campbell ancestors in the Kilmun Mausoleum near the Holy Loch. No cremation for Niall was possible with his high church views. He disliked cremation and said none of his ancestors had practised it, though in fact, his aunt, Princess Louise, chose to be cremated.[87]

CHAPTER 7
LOST TIMES RECALLED

As a child, I recall the ruddy-cheeked ferryman, Hope McArthur ("Hopie"), who would take passengers from St Catherine's to Inveraray and back again. His ferry was little more than a large rowing boat with an outboard motor, but, rain or shine, whether the loch was crystal clear or iced over, Hopie would cross the loch three times a day. The locals firmly believed the ferry unsinkable despite its frail appearance because Hopie instilled confidence. Hopie was the symbol of courage, resilience, and determination. He belonged to a clan which claimed descent from the legendary King Arthur, and though this clan shared the same roots as the Campbells, the MacArthur's proud boast in the Gaelic was "As old as the hills, the MacArthers and the devil." In early times, the clan's seat was at Strachur on Loch Fyne.

Inveraray Castle, Inveraray, across Loch Fyne from St Catherine's

The famous US General Douglas MacArthur had ancestors who came from Achnatra on Loch Fyne. In World War II he said, "I shall return" and did return to the Philippines. More recently still, another MacArthur, Eoin, contributed greatly to our knowledge of the people who have gone before us on the Cowal side of that loch with his book *Return to Loch Fyne*.

James I had the MacArther chief killed, so, in time, the MacArthur clan yielded supremacy in Argyll to the rising Campbells, whose chief shifted his castle from Loch Awe to Inveraray.

The quay where Hopie's ferry arrived at St Catherine's was once called the Ferry Inn. The Campbell earls of Argyll, with their retinues, would come over from Inverarary to St Catherine's and take their horses through Hell's Glen to Lochgoilhead, the original seat of the Ardkinglass Campbells, on their way to the lowlands.

As described here, after the Ardkinglass Campbell lairds came the Callanders, whose lives were enjoined by those of the volatile Erskines. Then, with the abrupt end to James Henry Callander's immediate family, Niall and Elspeth Campbell alone carried the Ardkinglass Campbell heritage until they died childless.

The period of 640 years is, as Niall Campbell wrote, "but a span in the lifetime of a planet," and "though the hills that keep watch, in their own unchanging silence, over the changing ownership of the glens, shall smile at the thought," such a period is only a fleeting moment in the march of time. New Loch Fyne industries have taken the place of old. Family initiatives, such as those of Douglas Campbell, have brought new life to Lochgoilhead with its recreational centre. The Glens of Loch Fyne have gained much from the enterprise of John and Michael Noble, who brought a new vitality to the Ardkinglass estate. The oyster business is now sustained and expanded by the work and dedication of the local community. But in all of this, let us not lose that sense of the past. Better yet, in the words of the Campbell motto, "ne oblivisceres" (do not forget).

Acknowledgements

The chart of the Campbells, Livingstons, Erskines, and Callanders was originally put together for me with painstaking attention and much skill by Duncan Findlay, the former editor of the *Link* magazine for the Lochgoilhead Kirk, and my immense gratitude goes to him. Graham Thomas, and more recently Andreas Michler and Mike Browne, did so much to further improve the images. Their desktop skills have been essential to this publication taking place at all as has the skilful work of Lee Goods and Jan Lewsey in getting this work completed.

My thanks also to those who have provided illustrations such as AJN from the Lochgoilhead Church and Jason Raftos for photographs across Loch Fyne. Also to Sandy Stevenson for the old photo of passenger steamer King Edward at Inveraray Pier.

Endnotes

Chapter 1: The Campbell Warriors of Ardkinglass

1. Map of Ardkinglass Campbell possessions
2. W. H. Murray, *The Companion Guide to the West Highlands of Scotland* Harper Collins Distribution Service (1968), 28.
3. Niall Diarmid Campbell letter to the Tenantry of Ardkinglass, Vigil of Xmas 1905.
4. Niall Campbell letter to tenantry 5.
5. Thomas Fulton, *The Sovereignty of the Sea: An Historical Account of the Sovereignty of the Sea (1911)*, Blackwood & Sons: Edinburgh & London 152—3. Later the Assize Herrings was commuted to a money payment. At p. 153 it is said that the Earle of Argyle rendered for Loch Fyne in 1613 to the King £36 as payment.
6. Niall Campbell letter to Tenantry, 6.
7. Records of letters of Treason against John Campbell 1594.
8. Niall Campbell letter to Tenantry, 7.
9. Niall Campbell letter to Tenantry., 7.
10. Niall Campbell letter to Tenantry, 7.
11. Niall Campbell letter to Tenantry, 9.
12. Duke Niall's letter to the Tenantry quoted in Sir Alistair Campbell, *A History of Clan Campbell: from Flodden to the Restoration* Vol. II, 171 Edinburgh: Edinburgh University Press 2002.
13. A charming but untrue story is that the wily Ardkinglass Campbell got Dunderave in his clutches by getting the Dunderave McNaughton drunk on his wedding night and thereby inducing him to wed his oldest Campbell daughter when McNaughton believed he was marrying the more attractive, younger daughter. McNaughton, later realising his error, eloped with the younger daughter, leaving Dunderave in Campbell's possession. The facts are more prosaic as explained by Angus McNaughton in *The Chiefs of the Clan McNaughton* (Oxley and Son (Windsor), 1951). The McNaughtons were in debt and chose the losing side in dynastic struggles.
14. Niall Campbell letter to Tenantry, 10.

Chapter 2: The Adventurer, James Callander of Craigforth and Ardkinglass

15. Sir James Campbell, *Memoirs of Sir James Campbell or Ardkinglass*, 2 vols. (London: Henry Colburn and Richard Bentley, 1832).
16. Sir James Campbell, *Memoirs of Sir James Campbell or Ardkinglass*, vol. 1. (London: Henry Colburn and Richard Bentley, 1832), 148–9.
17. Ibid., 228–9
18. Campbell, *Memoirs*, vol. 2, 240.
19. Campbell, *Memoirs*, vol. 1, 184–5.
20. Campbell, *Memoirs*, vol. 2, 205.
21. Ibid., 207.
22. Campbell, *Memoirs*, vol. 1, 259.
23. Ibid., 289.

24. Ibid., 325.
25. Ibid., 329.
26. Ibid., 379–383
27. Campbell, *Memoirs,* vol. 2, 31.
28. Campbell, *Memoirs,* vol. 1, 254; Vol. 2, 337.
29. Campbell, *Memoirs,* vol. 1, 292.
30. Ibid., 325.
31. Ibid., 325.
32. Campbell, *Memoirs,* vol. 2, 226.
33. Ibid., 254.
34. Ibid., 279, 347.
35. Niall Campbell to Tenantry, 10.
36. Campbell, *Memoirs,* vol. 2, 117.

Chapter 3: Three Erskine Brothers

37. Lt Colonel Ferguson, *Henry Erskine* (Blackwood & Sons, 1882), Edinburgh & London 204.
38. From Benjamin Franklin to Buchan, 17 March 1783, about Buchan buying land in America. Founders Online National Archives quoted from the papers of Benjamin Franklin Vol. 39 21 January to 15 May 1783 Ed. Ellen R Cohn New Haven & London Yale University Press 2008 pp 346-347.
39. From Jefferson to Buchan, 10 July 1803, Washington Papers. Founders Online National Archives from the papers of Thomas Jefferson Vol. 40. 4 March – 10 July 1803 Ed. Barbara Obemo Princetown University Press 2013 pp 711 – 712.
40. Buchan to Washington, 28 July 1791; Washington to Buchan, 1 May 1792. Founders Online National Archives from the papers of George Washington Presidential Series Vol. 8 22 March 1791 to 22 September 1791 Ed. Mark Mastra Marino Charlottesville; University Press of Virgina 1999 pp 305-308; Vol. 10. 1 March 1792 to 15 August 1792 Ed. Robert Haggard and Mastro Marino Charlottesville; University of Virginia 2000 pp 330 – 331.
41. Ferguson, *Henry Erskine,* 490–491.
42. John Lockhart, *Memoirs of the Life of Sir Walter Scott,* 1838 Paris & New York Public Library Press vol. 4, 204 (diary notes).
43. Ferguson related details of Deacon Brodie's trial and Henry Erskine's defence of him in *Henry Erskine,* 300–312.
44. *Dictionary of National Biography,* Erskine Henry vol. 17, 412 DJVU 418.
45. *Life of Lord Jeffery* 3rd Ed. Lexden Publishing Ltd: Essex Vol. 1 p. 91 by Henry Cockburn.
46. Ferguson, *Henry Erskine,* 103.
47. Ferguson, *Henry Erskine,* 96.
48. *Dictionary of National Biography,* vol. 17, 412–418 and cited in notes and queries vol. 10 7 July 1866 at 9.
49. Patrick Devlin: the Judge Oxford New York Melbourne Oxford University Press 1979 at p. 121.
50. Patrick Devlin at 121
51. Lord Campbell, *Lives of the Chancellors: Life of Thomas Erskine* 1859 4th Ed. Vol. VIII London John Murray 223-224.
52. J.A. Lovat-Fraser, *Erskine* (Cambridge University Press, 1932) 9, 10 & 37.
53. J.A. Lovat-Fraser, *Erskine* (Cambridge University Press, 1932) at 27
54. Campbell: Lives of the Chancellors Vol. VIII 289.
55. Baron Thomas Erskine, *Speeches of Thomas Lord Erskine* (Andesite Press, 1880), 225–6.
56. *Memoirs of the Life of Sir Walter Scott,* by John Lockhart vol. 4, 204 citing Sir Walter Scott's diary.
57. Ferguson, *Henry Erskine,* 483.
58. Ferguson, *Henry Erskine,* 491. (See also the meeting of the Whig Club when toasts were made to this effect, referred to at p. 475.)

Chapter 5: Lady Elspeth Campbell: The Fairy Godmother

59. The Otago Witness: "Lady's Gossip".
60. Jehanne Wake, *Princess Louise* (Collins,1988) London, 307–308.
61. In Ellen Terry's diary of April 14, 1897, she says, "Princess Louise (Lorne) came to see the play and told me she was delighted. Little Elspeth Campbell with her looking lovely."
62. *The Lore of Scotland: A Guide to Scottish Legends* 2009 Random House Books: London by Westwood & Kingshall.
63. *Proceedings of Society of Antiquarians of Scotland*, vol. 78, 1943–44, 141.
64. Rae MacGregor wrote an article for the *Oban Times* about Elspeth dated 4 January 1996. My mother, Janey Sevilla Lindsay, also referred to these features of Elspeth.
65. Jehanne Wake, *Princess Louise,* 382.
66. John Splendid 1898 Blackwood & Sons 4th Ed. Edinburgh & London at 77.
67. Neil Munro's short story "The Lost Pibroch and other Sheiling Stories" 1996 House of Lochar 2, places Halftown at an undefined point on the northern side of Loch Fyne. However, the St Catherine's hamlet has the Gaelic name Leth Bailie meaning Halftown. Furthermore, Isabella Douglas, in *History of Strachur,* tells of two pipers meeting to play the lost pibroch at the St Catherine's Halftown in very similar circumstances to that given by Neil Munro.
68. This is a translation from the Gaelic. Rose Forbes never married. Evan McColl, who lived at Kenmore near Inveraray, had a large family and migrated to Canada.
69. The Literature of the Highlands by Magnus McClean 1903 Blackie & Sons; London 183-190

Chapter 6: Niall Campbell (the Tenth Duke of Argyll)

70. Royal Commission on Ancient Monuments of Scotland, *Argyll: An Inventory of the Monuments,* vol. 7: Mid Argyll and Cowal, 199 (sketch at para 93).
71. Diaries of Neil Campbell 21 August 2013
72. Iain Moncrieffe, *The Highland Clans 1968: London* (Barrie & Rockliff). In the foreword, Moncrieffe speaks of Duke Niall's scholarly life work being sadly unpublished and therefore wasted. This is an effort to remedy that loss at least in small part.
73. Charles Lindley, "The Harper of Inveraray" in *Lord Halifax's Ghost Book,* 2nd ed. 1936 (Geoffrey Bles). 3–8.
74. Family collection - Duke Niall to Florence Sevilla Glass Hooper (nee Erskine), 16 January 1934.
75. Family collection - Duke Niall to Florence Sevilla, 31 August 1939.
76. Family collection - Duke Niall to Florence Sevilla, 9 November 1939.
77. Family collection - Duke Niall lost his cousin, Lieutenant Ivar Campbell (born May 1890, died 8 January 1916) in the First World War. Ivar was the son of Lord George Granvill Campbell, who was the son of the eighth duke of Argyll by Lady Elizabeth Leveson-Gower. I am grateful to Mr Alec Briggs for this information.
78. Family collection Rae McGregor, who worked at Inveraray Castle, kindly gave me a note of Niall's advising the donors of his wish to connect up the bell tower to the church. This did not occur.
79. Family collection - Duke Niall to Florence Sevilla, 25 January 1931.
80. Family collection - Duke Niall to Florence Sevilla, Whit Tuesday 1931.
81. Family collection - Duke Niall Niall to Florence Sevilla, 17 May 1931.
82. Family collection - Duke Niall to Florence Sevilla, 12 September 1931.
83. Family collection - Duke Niall to Florence Sevilla, 27 September 1932.
84. Family collection - Duke Niall to Florence Sevilla, 27 May 1933.
85. Family collection - Duke Niall to Florence Sevilla, 27 April 1937.
86. Family collection - Duke Niall to Florence Sevilla, 13 April 1937.
87. Jehanne Wake, *Princess Louise,* 412 (citing Niall's diary of 4 December 1939)

ABOUT THE AUTHOR

The author spent his childhood on the shores of Loch Fyne, in the heart of the Campbell country in the Scottish Highlands. His mother inherited lands from a Campbell Godmother which had once belonged to the Ardkinglass Campbells for over 760 years. He discovered in the attic of the house he inherited from his mother a treasure trove of letters, photos and personal effects from which the author tells of the turbulent history of the Ardkinglass family and the colourful and gifted descendants of that family, who played a large part in the social, artistic and political life of not only the Western Highlands but also Britain. The author is a lawyer who has written for the Spectator and Legal Journals, practicing law as a barrister at different times in London, Belize, Fiji, Adelaide and Perth in Australia. He returns each year to the Scottish Highlands.

Printed in the United States
By Bookmasters